155 SONNETS

by Willie Watson

Published in 2014
Prague, Czech Republic

also by Willie Watson:
Pink Snow (cover art by Daniela Šafránková)
Rheets
Twoems
What Do Children Like to Do? (with Lenka Brožová)
Uncle Willie´s Very Silly Animal Poems
The This of the That
Tarot Poems (with Marie Brožová)
The Alchemist´s Notebook
Four Syllables on Water
The Guru Kalehuru and Other Poems
Poems from Prague

Table of Contents

Introduction

A poem should have three things: rhyme, meter, and meaning. I have occasionally tried skipping the first two, the way most poets nowadays do, but I've never been happy with the results. It's never something I feel satisfied with; it doesn't feel poem-like to me.

Sonnets, archaic though they might be, have these three elements, so it's natural that I've dabbled in this form from time to time. After a few years in Prague, attending open mike (I know I'm swimming against the current with that spelling. I've got my reasons.) poetry readings on a regular basis, I thought "Damn, I must have written about a hundred sonnets by now. It would be cool to produce a collection of 155 of them, one more than Shakespeare." Yeah, I'm a nerd.

It would be a unique accomplishment, topping a record which nobody else is even trying to top,and which I'm not even sure is a record at all. In fact, I know for certain of a couple of people who've written more 'sonnets' than I have, but one frequently disregards the rule about rhyme, and the other one just throws rhyme and all the other rules right out the window, so I reckon I still win.

Anyway, I counted them up at that point and I'd actually only written about 35 or so. Still, I thought, I can do it if I crank up my game. After all, the human mind is basically a sonnet writing machine, if you adjust it to that setting. It takes in the raw material, which is the language itself, chops it up into lines of 10 syllables, matches the ones that rhyme, and after a bit more honing, rearranging, and stacking, voila, a bunch of sonnets pop out. Easy peasy. Yeah, right.

Ten years and millions of moments of self doubt later, the collection is complete, and here it is.

I'd like to write a few words of introduction about some of these poems individually; although I'm confident they all can stand on their own as far as meaning goes. The first 3 poems are the oldest, and were written while I was taking a course in Shakespeare at a community college. It was a fun class. The girl who was the inspiration for sonnet #3, The Huntress, was totally unimpressed, by the way. Poetry as a means of seduction is highly over-rated.

Two of the poems: Sonnet #18, The Uniform Texture of the Human Race, and Sonnet #54, Speed of Travel, were inspired by short stories written by Czech artist Marie Brožová, from her book The Souls of Trees, which I had the honor of helping with the translation of.

Three of the poems in this book are elegies. One for my father, one for Nelson Mandela, and Sonnet 61 for a kid named Alex Barber, who was well known on the Prague poetry circuit at the time I started out. He was also a musician and an actor. I asked him once how he could go so nuts on stage while still keeping things under control, and he said "That's not me up there. I just open myself up and let the spirit move through me." He lived fast and died too young, of a drug overdose, but that advice has stuck with me.

Sonnet #79, Rinat's Poem, is based on a poem by a friend of mine, Rinat Magsumov. He handed it to me and asked me to read it through and give him an opinion. I'm afraid I overdid it a bit and completely rewrote the poem. The original idea was his, but I left out lots of detailed information about cardiology, selenology and the role of flowers in the ecosystem. Rinat's a brainy guy, but it wouldn't have fit in this format.

Some of the poems here have appeared previously in other collections. Walking Through Nusle at Night, The Legend of Libuše, Logos and Theos, and Millenium all (Sonnets 57 through 60) are from my first book, Poems from Prague. Elegy for Alex and A Beautiful Mind (61 and 62) were in The Guru Kalehuru and Other Poems. Sonnet #127, A Single Grain of Sand, was in The Alchemist's notebook, as were Binary Lives, Democracy, Danger in the Grass, Empty Nests, Fading Conversations, 5 a.m., Phantom Map, Poem Without Clichés,The Moving Gallery, Parallell Tracks, Mid-Life Crisis, Points on a Line, Geometry,Soliliquy, Reciprocation,The Cynic, Rinat's Poem (mentioned above), Dandelions, and Sam at 5 months, and you can look them up. The Choice, is also from that book.

I don't feel I'm double dipping too egregiously, because this book contains plenty of Sonnets which have never found their way into print before and all of those books contain many other fine poems.

So, they are done. My challenge is met, my goal fulfilled, and I am quite pleased with myself, to tell you the truth.

Whether they are any good or not is up to you to judge.

Willie Watson

April 14th

The modern world calls out for modern words
And modern words fall into modern rhymes
The message from the medium is inferred
The words we choose speak plainly of our times

While singing songs of post industrial gloss
Our Rock and Rappin' rhythms seemed to fit
Yet truth is truth the universe across
And love and beauty haven't changed a bit

Five billion people people now the Earth
Live lives of jubilation and despair
Four more than at the time of Shakespeare's birth
Yet, I can't think of one I would compare

His language, so expressive and sublime
Still speaks to us across the space of time

Cleopatra

The younger love that's borne upon a glance
And buffeted on zephyrous winds of chance
It may as easy disappear as grow
Time will tell, and future ages know

But love that's fruit of two well-grafted vines
Two actors that know each the other's lines
Has gained in strength what it has lost in ease
It can't just drift away upon the breeze

Can never drift away, yet still could die
As cooler glances transforms the loving eye
Familiarity sows the seeds of scorn
Unless that love is constantly reborn

Though love may last as long as life is long
It's only when that love itself stays strong

The Huntress

The woman who's both beautiful and bright
A huntress grown disdainful of her game
Draws men, like moths, unto her beauty's flame
But sees us all too clearly in that light

The woman thus endowed will soon suspect
As she becomes the object of men's eyes
Her thoughts are not the subject of their sighs
But beauty is the means that's more direct

Yet, it cannot be a crime to be a man
And follow nature's clearly posted way,
And sway with winds were meant to make us sway
And love as men have loved since time began

There's no apology we need to make
For loving beauty just for beauty's sake

Urban Wilds

I took a walk around my neighborhood
A sunny day and everything was good
A random turn and suddenly I saw
A place where I had never been before

Abandoned, derelict and overgrown
Some trees, some flowers, some garbage and some stones
Behind a supermarket, sort of blocked
From view and so I was a little shocked

Out into space and underneath the sea
We see so far when watching our TV
Around each corner and behind each door
For everything we see, there's so much more

No matter where we are, or where we go
There are so many things that we don't know

Fractals Revealed

Great rivers start as rivulets and streams
Which carve the landscape everywhere they go
A moving template for an artist's dreams
The changing rhythm of their steady flow

Nothing's random, everything conforms
To nature's constant law, it never fails
The movement of the stars, the growth of storms
Each flowers petals, swirling shells of snails

The mighty trees (which grew from tiny seeds)
Stretch their arms into the endless sky
Each branch's twigs are thick as garden weeds
From which the flocks of birds take off and fly

From large to small is how the branches grow
From small to large is how the rivers flow

Crown Jewels

The tourists stand in never ending lines
To see the gems of long forgotten kings
An endless fascination with such things
Lies deep within the caverns of our minds

They marked the wealth of those who ruled the Earth
The colors are both beautiful and bold
The emeralds so green, the amber gold
Their beauty's more than equal to their worth

POWER, power is flowing from the Sun
Every day we're basking in its glow
It helps the flowers and the trees to grow
It shines; it shines on each and every one

The wealth of man is growing all around
And more is growing upward from the ground

New Tech, Old Emotions

Poems are a reflection of their times
And, of course, of all the times before
Ancient words rewrit in modern rhymes
Each generation gives a little more

There are some themes that are, forever, true
Love and lust, desire and jealousy
But there are always some things that are new
New concepts, fashions and technologies

Shakespeare never sent an SMS
Shelley couldn't access online porn
Wordsworth never used the internet
They were long dead before these things were born

Things have changed, and they will change again
But what we feel is what they felt back then

Walking on Earth

My feet are quite attracted to the ground
It's work to even lift them up and then
Sledge hammer fashion, they come dropping down
And then, the process can begin again

Quite opposite to that, there is my head
It sits upon my neck quite easily
And so it goes wherever it is led
And breathes the air, which blows so breezily

The sky goes up and up until it's blue
And turns to black when it is late at night,
Up close, it is invisible, it's true
Because of some strange trickery of light

We're planted on the Earth, the Earth spins round
The sky is everything above the ground

A Different Interpretation

It's in the bible, Seek and Ye Shall Find
Matthew 7:7, to be precise
If you don't look, you might as well be blind
Generally, it's pretty good advice

If you're at home, just sitting in your chair
You will not see the lilacs in the park
The waterfalls and castles everywhere
You'll never see a rainbow in the dark

But ...if you're seeking that which isn't there
The act of seeking causes it to be
Magic worlds and castles in the air
There are so many things that you might see

The mind is strange, and subject to confusion
The quest for truth can lead to self-delusion

Reconnection

The people who we knew from way back when
When we were kids, when we were troubled youth
Idealistic, radical young men
Wild eyed hippies looking for the truth

And when we traveled round the world we met
Some people here, some other people there
We were friends, and sometimes lovers, yet
We then grew worlds apart, and unaware

But now we live part time in cyberspace
Now and again, we meet these friends of old
And usually we find that it's the case
They've gained some weight; they've gone a little bald

But they are living fairly normal lives
Houses, pets and children, husbands and wives

On Rivers and Fountains

The fountains that we see in public squares
Every major city has a few
Send up a mighty spray and clear the air
They're beautiful and rather useful, too

They are a pleasant spot for friends to meet
For tourists just to snap a couple shots
For kids to splash in, in the summer heat
There's a lot that happens in these spots

But also, almost every city's set
Upon a river's banks, or on the shore
Of lake, or bay, or mighty ocean, yet
We always feel we need a little more

I love to sit and watch a fountain's spray
But a river can still carry you away

It's in the Meter

Poetry's a rhythmic form of speech
The lines are a specific, matching length
Each line is weighted, at the end of each
There's a rhyme, and that's the poem's strength

Table Tennis is a pleasant game
Conversation isn't an attack
The oarsmen in a boat all row the same
Dip together, pull, then lift, then back

Poetry's a form of intercourse
The Yin and Yang, each ping inspires a pong
And as our thoughts get echoed, back and forth
A simple set of words becomes a song

A dance, a chant, a ritual, a spell
Poetry's like magic, when done well

Appropriate Means of Locomotion

They spread their wings and drift upon the air
As easy as we walk upon the ground
Each in his place, so it is only fair
We each have our own way to get around

The sky above's a sullen sort of gray
And there are puddles on the ground, but yet
It is a rather pleasant sort of day
The world is very pretty when it's wet

Now and then we get a bit frustrated
With stupid things that people say and do
Life is difficult and complicated
It is for me, I'm sure it is for you

Relax. Don't struggle. You don't have to try.
Look at the birds –how easily they fly

Lucien's Poem

Everything that's wood was once a tree
I read those words and felt that they were fine
There is a string of continuity
contained within the wood, and in those lines

The windowpane was once a pile of sand
The steel was just another bit of stone
Everything has come up from the land
the homes we live in, everything we own

But somewhere, there's a line that we have crossed
We've stripped the Earth, and nearly left it bare
In memory of the paradise we've lost
we have the table, and we have the chair

So, when you feel that things have gone off track
Touch something, and just let it all come back

Cavemen and Us

We aren't so very different, in some ways
From those who lived a million years ago
They had the clouds, the rain, the wind, the snow
Starry nights and long, hot summer days

They liked to talk, to laugh, to eat, to sing
To sleep when they were tired and to eat
(Although they lived on nuts and scavenged meat)
And copulation was their favorite thing

There was no way that they could then foresee
Telescopes in space, computer games
But their urges and desires were the same
They were the seed of what we've come to be

We aren't so very different from them
Though what is new to us was then unknown
They had some revolutions of their own
Plus ca change, plus ca reste la měme

In many ways, we're similar enough
But, certainly, we have much cooler stuff

Redefining Magic

A movie wizard says a word or two
And suddenly there's food on every plate
We all say aaaah and think that would be great
But is it really something we can't do?

Just put a tiny seed into the ground
It takes a while, but eventually
That little seed becomes a mighty tree
Where bright and shining globes of fruit abound

The words we write are like a magic spell
The music, which is sculpted from thin air
Is a chant, an incantation or a prayer
To call on heaven or raise a little hell

We're in a magic world, but unaware
Just because it seems so ordinary

Erosion of Intent

I admire William Blake, he was...divine
He penned deservedly immortal lines
Alas, no matter how hard one might try
Symmetry just doesn't rhyme with eye

I don't know for sure, but I suspect
That in his day, and in his dialect
They did- but with the steady flow of time
There has been an erosion of the rhyme

As brand new concrete soon is black with dust
And gleaming steel eventually will rust
The warm spring rain consumes the snowman's flesh
There is no fruit that stays forever fresh

No matter how well formed, or full of wit
Time will pass, and turn our words to shit

The Uniform Texture of the Human Race

A field of snow, a gently rising slope
A sea of white, its billows calm and still
it's uniformly beautiful, until
we take a look into a microscope

They're individuals! Unique and proud
Each flake of snow presents a different face
these complex fractals, drawn in frozen lace
a trillion different faces in the crowd

We have our individuality
But if beings came from outer space
To investigate the human race
That is not the first thing that they'd see

What they'll think is really hard to know
But we are not as clean and pure as snow

Letnany

The world comes into focus upside down
Revealed in steps, each step along the way
As we exit from the underground
And step into the lucid light of day

First, the sky above comes into view
Some days it's blue, some days it's sullen gray
When we come out at night, the stars shine through
Like signals from a billion miles away

Then, the buildings–first, the upper floors
Then the rows of windows moving down
Finally, the sidewalks and the doors
Then we're back on the surface, back in town

As we move from point to point, it's not so strange
At certain points, our point of view will change

Pacengo

There are some perfect beaches made of sand
Others are grass, and some are made of stone
The surface cover is what sets the tone
In the place where the water meets the land

At Pacengo, the beach is made of shells
The skeletons of things that were alive
In this placid lake, these creatures thrived
I'm not surprised, I also liked it well

They had the water, and they had the sun
They ate, they grew, they bred and then they died
Their inert corpses drifted to one side
Washed up on the shore when they were done

A place for me to place my towel and lie
In the sun and let my body dry

Time is an Onion

In events sequentially unfolding
We measure out this thing that we call time
The petals drop, the secrets they were holding
Are revealed, the process is sublime

The water that is gushing from the fountains
Looks almost solid in its symmetry
The tiny trickle high up in the mountains
Flows in a steady stream down to the sea

Children grow and some of them have children
But then we all get old and fade away
Generation follows generation
And kids are always pretty much the same

So it has been, so it will always be
Existence is in continuity

View From the Pont D'Arve, Geneva

The river winds, as rivers tend to do
(a pattern that is generally thanks
To gradual erosion of their banks)
In nature, straight is not the same as true

I wonder what is just around the bend
What rocks, what flowers, what houses and what trees?
The void is full of possibilities
I'm curious, although I know they tend

To be in some particulars the same
A house must be a house, a tree a tree
There are some limits to what things can be
The picture never goes outside the frame

But then, there is the bend around the bend
And then, and then, and still...it never ends

Flying Bikes

I see the bicycles sailing through the sky
(Attached to the roof of a car, I know)
A hedge obscures my view, and so they fly
It makes me wonder where they'd like to go

These progeny of Pegasus have wheels
Which are, in some ways, just as good as wings
There's a sense of freedom that you feel
There's a sense of happiness it brings

Sure, when they arrive, they'll be unbound
Of course, they cannot literally fly
Their wheels will be in contact with the ground
But the rider's head is in the sky

The pedals start to turn, the wheels to spin
And the rider turns his face into the wind

Beads

It's so much fun to string the little beads
Orange and yellow, green and blue and red
No limit to the possibilities
The ways they can be ordered on the thread

Chess, a game of tactics, must be played
Upon a board that's eight small squares by eight
And yet, the different moves that can be made
Are nearly infinite, they are that great

The markers in a strand of DNA
The winds unscripted music on the chimes
Red and orange, yellow, green and gray
The sequence will be different every time

Infinite variations on a theme
Poems, snowflakes, human beings and dreams

Consumer Society

While walking through the park one day so fair
I saw some rubbish lying on the ground
And wondered why it should be lying there
When there were rubbish bins placed all around

It makes me mad, there ought to be a law
People are like pigs and always throwing
Their garbage everywhere, but then I saw
All the bins were filled to overflowing

The candy bars, the ice cream and the chips
Everything we eat we first unwrap
The world's become a giant rubbish tip
And what's left over is a lot of crap

When I see how much people can consume
I truly think the human race is doomed

The Sea and the Night

The sea is vast and goes the whole world round
And there are many people it has drowned
The sea is frightening to you and me
But not so scary if you are the sea

When you go for a walk outside at night
The day is gone, and with it's gone the light
The lines are blurred and all you see and hear
Is colored by the things you truly fear

But look out at the universe at night,
That's speckled with a million tiny lights
The sea, the night, the never ending dark
Illuminated with a billion sparks

The sea, the night, the universe are one
And nothing in the chain can be undone

Above the Church

A flock of birds that's surfing on the breeze
So elegant, so beautiful, so free
And what they do they do with such great ease
They are a living form of poetry

The choreography is sweetly planned
No humans ever work as such a group
They wheel as one, and climb and turn and swoop
More synchronized than any marching band

And yet, they are such tiny little things
Whose brains are not much bigger than a pea
Although they soar upon their outstretched wings
It's not, to them, a flight of fantasy

We look up at the birds and are amazed
To them, it's just an ordinary day

The Difference Between Man and the Animals

Though animals have eyes with which to see
They taste their food, and feel the things they touch
And ears to hear, the same as you and me
And sense the world around them just as much

As any human being in this room
They do not tend to dwell upon the past
Or moan about their own impending doom
They live their lives as long as they may last

Like us, they see the stars in outer space
But do not know that they are balls of fire
Though we admire their innocence, and grace
On evolution's scale, we are the higher

The past, the future, distant worlds unknown
Are the realms of human beings alone

The Second Coming of the Snow

The snow is falling softly on the ground
Just as soft as anyone could please
And as it falls, it doesn't make a sound
And some lands on the branches of the trees

The snow can be a metaphor for life
Its silence can be louder than a song
It's lovely, it's pristine, it's very nice
But doesn't stay the same for very long

The sky is clear and now the snow has stopped
In puffs and chunks upon the ground below
The stuff that's on the branches starts to drop
It is the second coming of the snow

As long as you're alive, and not in jail
You've got your second chance, try not to fail

Touchstone Days

At Hallowe'en, you see the pumpkin's leer
Reminding you of Hallowe'ens gone by
That ghastly smile's the same in every year
Among the autumn leaves so brown and dry

At Christmas you will see the brilliant lights
And remember your sweet child's joy
The way his eyes grew large and shined so bright
At the opening of a brand new toy

Easter's eggs, the fireworks in July
For most of us, spark memories quite pleasant
Reminding us of holiday's gone by
A happy link between the past and present

But to a parent who has lost a child
These touchstone days will bring more tears than smiles

My Favorite Zoo Animal

I like to watch the primates in the zoo
Because they are so much like me and you
Their curling fingers love to grab and clutch
And they'll hold on to anything they touch

And they are often hesitant to share
Anything that they perceive as theirs
They fight - they are competitive as hell
But they can have a softer side as well

The mothers hold their babies to their breasts
And for that one they would fight all the rest
The little ones just love to run and play
Instinctively, they know to seize the day

I like to watch them swinging in the trees
Because they are so much like you and me

One Important Aspect of Rhyme

As a poet, I confess, I am a hack
While some express their thoughts, I juggle words
And hope that, in the end, a thought is spurred
Just as a train must stay upon the track

The wild river flows between two banks
The picture cannot go outside the frame
There are boundaries in every game
The sheep must have the sheepdog at their flanks

Not everything that's written has to rhyme
In fact, sometimes it sounds contrived and wrong
A novel cannot keep it up for long
Haiku is short and simple and sublime

There are many styles, we all know ,em
But if it rhymes, you know it is a poem

Mutual Evolution

We have evolved within this atmosphere
This envelope of air, this tiny shell
Around the planet we all know so well
We know so well, of course, because we're here

The rivers flow with water we can drink
The plants that grow are good for us to eat
The surface is well suited to our feet
It couldn't be more perfect, I don't think

Yet, as we find new planets out in space
Each one is very different from our own
Fiery hells or frigid, barren stone
Although life could evolve in other places

On different planets, under other skies
The phrase "life as we know it" won't apply

The Imaginary Artist

I've always been an artist in my mind
Because I can see faces in the clouds
And when I see these pictures in the sky
For some strange reason that makes me feel proud

That I am so perceptive and aware
That in these shapes which shift so fluidly
I can see a world that isn't there
And that is an amazing thing to see

But when I try to tell you what I've seen
It doesn't sound like very much at all
There's a face, and over there's a tree
It's just a picture on a big, blue wall

An artist is someone who can convey
That other world in painting, sculpture, sound
In words, perhaps, there are so many ways
To represent the images you've found

I've always been an artist in my mind
But that's not where an artist is defined

If a Tree Falls....

If a tree that's in a lifeless forest
Falls down and makes an imprint on the ground
Far away from life's incessant chorus
Actually, it doesn't make a sound

When I write a poem I'm really trying
To write down every thought that's in my head
But that's only half, there's no denying
That they are incomplete if they're unread

The words we write don't all get passed along
But they are placed within the growing pile
Of all the shit on Amazon.com
A silent archive of expanding files

Billions and billions and billions of words
Which stay unread, that is to say, unheard

Chicken or Egg

The chicken or the egg, which one came first
It's a conundrum and a paradox
The hen lays eggs, containing hens and cocks
When the yolk's no longer funny, out they burst

But dinosaurs laid eggs long, long before
A chicken ever sat upon a nest
To put philosophers to such a test
And there are many other creatures more

Amphibians and reptiles, frogs and snakes
The lowliest of creatures can lay eggs
Even fish, who haven't any legs
They're unevolved, but have the stuff it takes

It's the egg, and please don't ask me that again
You're giving too much credit to the hen

Anonymity

The people who are on the moving stairs
Are moving in a never ending line
There is no way to know what's on their minds
Their faces give no hint of their affairs

And when they're in their cars we see still less
There's nothing that might give the slightest clue
How old they are or what they like to do
We can't see what they look like, how they're dressed

Each one a drop within a mighty stream
And when you go online, it's even more
Each voice subsumed within the mighty roar
Of faceless fans all cheering for the team

While on the quest for anonymity
We lose our individuality

Cemeteryville

We marvel at the beauty of the reef
A cemetery deep beneath the sea
Where tiny little corals came to grief
And this is what their bodies came to be

As I walk down this ancient city's streets
And try to know this ancient city's heart
I see how it's complex but still complete
A jigsaw puzzle made of many parts

How many people worked until they died?
Hearts and minds dressed up in skin and bone
To build this monument to human pride
Stacking bricks and carving things in stone

Centuries of work is quite a price
For us to look and say "that's very nice."

God's Big Stone

The question has been posed, can God create
A stone of such great density and weight
Or perhaps of such great size around
That he himself can't lift it from the ground

Since mankind first conceived of deities
About the time we came down from the trees
We've used them to explain this world of ours
The wind and rain were godly magic powers

Then came language, civilization, science
Brilliant new inventions and appliances
How much more advanced can we all get
Now that we have got the internet?

The question about God is moot, because
Humble homo sapiens can, and does

Lobsters in a Pot

If you put just one lobster in a pot
The chances are that he will get away
When the water starts to get too hot
There is little reason he should stay

But there's a simple thing that you can do
To secure your succulent seafood snack
Just add another lobster to the stew
When one climbs up, the other pulls him back

People are a bit like that at times
In the city, in the country, in the town
Whenever they see someone start to climb
They reach right out and try to drag him down

If you want to go beyond the comfort zone
You just might have to make it on your own

Back to School

New born babies are one of life's great joys
But, Jesus Christ!, they make a lot of noise
They cry, they poop, they poop, they cry, they cry
And there are moments when we wonder why

We thought it would be fun to reproduce
As we suffer through an earful of abuse
We eagerly await that golden day
When we can send the little brats away

Today, there is a cool and pleasant breeze
The leaves are brown and falling from the trees
It's time to send the children off to school
That's the schedule, the tradition and the rule

Every year we see the seasons change
We should not be surprised, it's not so strange
The green of summer wasn't meant to last
It fades into the sweet nostalgic past

It's natural and always has been so
Autumn is the time for letting go

The Dawn of Intellectual Curiosity

The naked apes began to walk the plains
A hundred thousand years ago or more
How odd it must have felt that they had brains
No creature had had such a thing before

Intellectual curiosity
Science and religion, magic and art
Long ago in the days of prehistory
No one thought to keep these fields apart

They painted pictures that were more than art
Pictures of the animals they killed
Magic and religion played a part
As the world became the subject of their will

How very strange existence must have seemed
When they slept, I wonder what they dreamed

Fading In

When we wake up, our dreams are bright and clear
But in a moment they all fade away
There are new sights to see and sounds to hear
After all, it is another day

Like the stars that shine from such a distance
Become invisible at break of dawn
The light of day rolls over all resistance
And the stars, in all their millions, are just gone

Those who had dreams of glory in their youth
Get lost in life, as every day they deal
With the very inconvenient truth
Life is, has been and always will be real

Dreams by day as well as dreams by night
Fade quickly when they are exposed to light

A Picture of the Wind

We look through a window and see a world
The grass, the trees, it all looks rather tame
Just the tiniest fractal is unfurled
Just that small bit within the window frame

We cannot see the wind, but we can see
The leaves that bow before it as it passes
The automatic unanimity
In the deferential movement of the grasses

Perhaps we see the traffic zipping by
But where they all are going, we can't say
Perhaps we see a field of pale blue sky
Which other times appears as somber gray

What we can see is just a tiny part
Of a vastly more expansive work of art

An Advantage to Social Media

When Robert's Rules of Order are applied
Opposing points of view can be discussed
We may not understand the other side
Or like them much, but deal with them we must

Of course, some people prattle on too long
They shout, they scream, they shake their fists in rage
The most verbose are usually most wrong
And yet they tend to dominate the stage

And that is why I love the written word
It's silent and does not offend the ear
It is, inside your head, distinctly heard
It isn't loud at all, but still it's clear

I write down all my thoughts and post the text
And then I wait to hear what you say next

Sky Sonnet

The passing airplane leaves a narrow trail
That marks the plotted course by which it flies
As straight and true as if it were on rails
Two white lines across the clear, blue sky

And if we were to follow those two lines
They would take us to some other place
Where there are different words on different signs
There are different people, different faces

We don't all dress, or look, or speak the same
Spaceship Earth has quite a motley crew
But we are like one picture, in one frame
Here underneath this dome of baby blue

The moving finger writes, and leaves it there
A line that is a link, up in the air

The Mirror

The glowing moon we think we see at night
Is, in reality, reflected light
The sun is far away, the moon is nearer
And so, it acts a little like a mirror

By day, we are immersed in light and heat
At night, the sun is shining more discreetly
The great, almighty sun has many ways
To spread and to perpetuate its rays

The speckled beams that shimmer on the sea
The chlorophyll that's in the grass and trees
Its energy's been spread both far and wide
So everybody has a light inside

Do not frown, and be oppressed by gloom
When you smile, there's sunshine in the room

The Problem of Overpopulation

There are 7 billion people on this Earth
The number is increasing every day
The deaths cannot keep pace with all the births
And usually, I think that that's O.K.

We love to touch a pregnant woman's belly
We're thrilled to hear a newborn infant's cry
When they smile, we all turn to jelly
But oh, we are so sad when someone dies

It's instinctive, this urge we have to breed
But very soon we will run out of space
And food, and other things that we all need
To make the world a pleasant sort of place

If we don't want the world to turn to shit
Perhaps we need to slow things down a bit

The Seven Billion

These 7 billion living, breathing souls
Have 7 billion different pairs of eyes
And so they see their 7 billion roles
In 7 billion very different ways

Each vision of the world is quite distinct
But there is love in 7 billion hearts
We will have conflict, but I also think
That we will have great music and great art

There are 7 billion pairs of hands
To make light work of all that must be done
And so I find it hard to understand
Why those hands should have to carry guns

If we all work together, we can thrive
But if we don't, then we may not survive

The Beat of Life

Every day at 9 a.m. he barks
An animated version of a clock
Piercing, sharp, staccato, loud and stark
The suburban version of a crowing cock

The tennis balls that fly across the court
Meet the racket with a sudden thwack
It's the drumbeat, it's the rhythm of the sport
As once again, the ball goes flying back

The breaking of the waves upon the shore
Shattering into a million drops
The opening and the closing of the doors
At every place the tram comes to a stop

Off and on, we all go on our way
In the rhythm of an ordinary day

Phantom Map

I wonder, if there were some sort of map
That led to a Utopia, somewhere
A perfect place, that's free of all the crap
That is the current state of world affairs

I wonder, if there were a microscope
So powerful that we could plainly see
A gleam of promise, or a ray of hope
That someday everybody would be free

I wonder, if there were a looking glass
So honest, it could see inside our minds
Below the surface; gender, race or class
I wonder if we'd like the things we'd find

If the answers were all written in a book,
Would we believe, or would we even look?

One Fine Autumn Day in Sady Svatopluka Cecha

The leaves are falling from the trees like snow
Almost as light as air, they fall real slow
They scratch the asphalt with a rasping sound
But fall quite silently on grassy ground

A scooter roars across the public green
And in its wake, it's churning up a mean
And angry cloud of chopped up leaves and dust
As the driver, and his boss, assume they must

But if he hadn't come to work at all
It would not, in any way, disturb the fall
The winter would still come, as we all know
And leave the leaves all covered up in snow

They'd decompose into the rich, black earth
In preparation for the spring's re-birth
That, of course, was always nature's plan
Which worked quite well, before the time of man

If we want the joy that nature brings
We don't need to do a single thing

Train of Thought

A train of thought, a stream of consciousness
Are things that spring, unbidden, from your mind
Both are accurate metaphors, I guess
For how everything is moving in a line

The stream pours out, a single, massive force
Unstoppable, a wave, a juggernaut
The train is more mechanical, of course
With links connecting each and every thought

The moving finger writes and having writ
Moves on and writes another line or two
Some of it is brilliant, some is shit
Hopefully, at least, it's something new

We think faster than we can write, or read
In particles and waves, our thoughts proceed

Speed of Travel

The view we see outside our moving train
Or from the window of our speeding car
Goes by so fast we cannot see it plain
But everything becomes a sort of blur

When you're on foot, each second is distinct
Each tree, each bush, each blade of grass, each stone
When you have time to contemplate, and think
Each moment forms an image of its own

And when the day is done and you reflect
On all the memories that you have got
A clear result is what you should expect
The slow exposure took the cleaner shot

Although it's true that speed gives us a thrill
We see more clearly when we're standing still

The Meaning of Life

We work, we play, we eat, we sleep, we dance
We talk, we sing, we read, perhaps we write
We love and we experience romance
We have some laughs but there are times we fight

Our time is filled with lots of different stuff
From when we're born, until the day we die
Of some of it we never get enough
But still, we sometimes stop and wonder...why?

We live our lives to our alloted span
Eighty, maybe ninety years or so
Although we do the very best we can
It's possible that we will never know

No matter how courageously we strive
Exactly what it means to be alive

Hrabovska Dolina

The streetlight shining on the placid lake
The water dancing in its steady lights
The streetlight is a camera which takes
A photographic negative of night

The cars continue driving in the dark
Their headlights bore two holes in the unknown
Slicing out a segment, clear and stark
To mark the path by which they need to go

The sunlight shining through the big glass door
To signal the beginning of the day
Casts a golden shadow on the floor
And anything that's sitting in the way

The light of day, so beautiful and fair
Is greater still at times when it is rare

Walking Through Nusle at Night

It's two a.m; I need to get some sleep
But the night bus is a half an hour away
I'd rather walk than stand around and wait
And so, at night, I walk the city streets

When all the trade and traffic of the day
Has disappeared and all the streets are clear
The static's gone away and we can hear
The click of shoes a block or two away

I feel compelled to silence and to stealth
The night is black in mourning for the day
And all that's bright has faded into gray
The city is a statue of itself

Each building is a piece of that design
And here and there a screen is glowing white
But the action's mostly hidden from our sight
The human drama plays for private eyes

It's only in the darkness of the night
We see the true significance of light

The Legend of Libuse

Between two sloping banks the river flowed
About a river deep and river wide
An ancient forest covered either side
One fall, a couple thousand years ago

One day, a princess walking through the wood
Ate some mushrooms growing from the ground
(The kind that make your head spin round and round)
Sat down on the bank and it was good

The evening sun so red it looked like fire
Belied the coolness of the evening breeze
And in the light it cast upon the trees
She saw a city of a thousand spires

Whose beauty reached up to the very sky
There by the river, with its steady flow
She sat and watched the golden city grow
And her vision was completed, by and by

How could Libuše so exactly see
The way things really did turn out to be?

Logos and Theos

In the woods, a tree falls to the ground
But no one's there, so does it make a sound?
If sounds defined as something that we hear
The answer must be negative, it's clear

If God created man, and not instead
The other way around, as some have said
It may have been because he had no choice
Does he exist if no one hears his voice?

From the seed, the reaching, looping vines
Never, ever grow along straight lines
Yet plants whose leaves are twisted, random, tangled
Are seen as fields with even lines and angles

From the mountains towering above
The pattern's only clear when you're clear of it
The credit for the universal plan
In fairness, must be shared by God and man

The Logos is connected to the Theos
What else but order could come out of chaos?

Millenium

We're spinning as we're turning round the sun
In 24 hours, each and every time
One year and then we're back where we began
It's a pattern, it's a system, it's a rhyme

About a hundred thousand years ago
We marked the seasons and we named the days
Planted seeds and stayed to watch them grow
And got a bit more settled in our ways

Began to shape the earth to our desires
Killed for profit - killed for power - killed for fun
Scarred the earth with fences and with fires
As year by year we turned around the sun

Somehow, we've managed to survive this far
The sun still shines upon us as we dance
Weak and undeserving though we are
Each day presents us with another chance

Spinning, spinning through the cosmic night
We've got another thousand years to get it right

Elegy for Alex

Here in this town where people come and go
You meet a lot of people passing through
Most leave no impression, but you know
Some make a mark, and one of them was you

You played on your guitar and sang your songs
The power of your voice could move a crowd
You sang with feeling and your voice was strong
It suited those of us who like it loud

As I'm walking down these cobbled streets
Or sitting in some smoky bar at night
I know that it will never be complete
I think of all the songs you'll never write

What does it mean, to say you died too young?
Is eighty years enough, or eighty five?
Most who live so long don't do as much
As you accomplished when you were alive

The songs you sang still echo in my head
Alex, I'm so sorry that you're dead

A Beautiful Mind

Most people find it difficult enough
To go to work each day and deal with things
Like traffic, bills and all the other stuff
That daily life inevitably brings

By concentrating on the daily grind
By diligence, and focussing too tight
We dull our senses, slowly we go blind
Or simply close our eyes against the light

Outgrow imaginary childhood friends
And leave the shores of never-never land
Instead of understanding to pretend
We accept, and then pretend to understand

Is it an aberration or a gift?
To see more than two sides to every coin
To float above the clouds, to catch the drift
Is that a poet...or a paranoid?

Self-delusion or a lucky flair?
For seeing things that aren't really there

Binary Lives

While walking past the panelaks at night
I notice that a few of them are dark
While some of them emit a brilliant light
The contrast in the images is stark

Some on, some off, that's all they ever show
Of the lives that people live inside
People I may never get to know
Some in, some out, and thus we are divided

Some are happy, some, no doubt, are sad
Some are sitting down to eat their dinner
Some are talking, some are getting mad
Some are losers, some of them are winners

Each screen tuned in to a different station
We all live our lives in isolation

Democracy

Democracy is such a lovely word
It means "The People Rule," in ancient Greek
A lovely thought, a worthy goal to seek
And to all other systems it's preferred

But "people" covers quite a lot of ground
The good, the bad, the ugly and the sick
Some ignorant, and some are just plain thick
I think that covers most of us around

The issues are complex, but we are not
And fail to really think the issues through
(The way the rulers really ought to do)
When a clever slogan fills the spot

As long as we, so easily, are fooled
We, the people, always will be ruled

Danger in the Grass

I've noticed that there are not any signs
In Prague's fair parks, through which I often pass
Warning of imprisonment or fines
If you should dare to step upon the grass

The grass is dark and thick, and getting long
But tourists learn, and locals are aware
That there are dangers lurking in the lawn
Placed like little land mines here and there

They're shaped a little like a fat cigar
The texture's like a squirmy sort of glue
Tread on the grass, you won't get very far
Before one finds the bottom of your shoe

Although the lawn looks sweet, and green, and nice
Stray from the path, and you will pay the price

Empty Nests

In summer when the leaves are thick and green
The forest is a dark and hidden place
And from outside the inside can't be seen
So dense that you can hardly find a trace

Of order, form, the structure of the plot
It doesn't want to give a thing away
The velvet curtain can conceal a lot
But somewhere near the climax of the play

The leaves fall to the ground, the curtains part
And so reveal the sights which were forbidden
The woven works of ancient avian art
The nests which once were quite demurely hidden

A shallow bowl, a small inverted dome
That is the birds abandoned summer home

Fading Conversations

At parties, or the clubs where we all go
The sacred places of the social scene
We talk with people who we barely know
And don't always say exactly what we mean

When someone says "How are you?" we say "Great"
"O.K.", "Not bad", "I really can't complain"
We do not pause, no need to hesitate
We're always ready with some old cliché

But then there comes a moment when it's still
We sip our drinks, as if our throats are dry
Conversation takes a bit of skill
And no one wants to be there when it dies

We make a lame excuse and walk away
When we can't think of anything to say

5 a.m.

I like to go out walking round the town
When everybody else is still in bed
Without the constant stream of city sounds
I can hear the thoughts inside my head

Without the hum of busses, trains and cars
The rat-tat-tat of drills against the walls
The conversations spilling from the bars
Without the phones, their different tones, their calls

The city seems so calm, and so composed
A scene that's as serene as it can be
Without the interference that's imposed
You can hear the birds up in the tree

The city would be wonderful, no doubt
If only all the people were kicked out

Poem Without Clichés

I'd like to write a poem without cliches
No stars that shine like pinpricks in the sky
No brooks that babble as they're rushing by
No children playing on hot summer days

To represent the innocence we've lost
For words, like bees, once used, have lost their sting
And used again, no longer mean a thing
They're like a bridge that we've already crossed

No rain that falls on lonely streets at night
As metaphor for life's unending pain
The weather's insufficient to explain
The depth of our emotions, and our plight

No hell below, no heaven up above
No birds that fly upon a gentle breeze
That whispers as it ruffles through the trees
No soaring hearts with wings to speak of love

I'd like to write a poem without that shit
Alas, I must confess, this wasn't it

The Moving Gallery

Looking out the window of the train
A moving window on a placid scene
There are things out there I can't explain
There are things I don't know what they mean

I see a tractor drive across the ground
I don't know what his plan is for that day
From where I sit, I cannot hear a sound
It's just a picture in a silent play

I see a castle standing on a hill
Once, it had great power in its grasp
But we move on, and it is standing still
Once again, receding in the past

I see a princess on the tower's top
Looking at the peasants down below
Walking through the fields and tending crops
One sunny day, one spring of long ago

The mind can drift; it will, in time, come back
It's just the train must stay upon the track

Parallel Tracks

The train is running on parallel tracks
It rolls across the earth and then it's gone
As far as the horizon and beyond
Na paralelních kolejích jede vlak

The mighty dragon crawls along the ground
A couple hundred tons of rolling steel
The clicking of a thousand tiny wheels
Racing forward, as they spin around

Riding in the belly of the beast
Like Jonah, in the belly of the whale
Each passenger can tell a different tale
And thus, the dragon's power is increased

I watch the trains as they go rumbling by
And wonder at the tales they have to tell
As countless other poets have, as well
Across the years, across the clear night sky

There are two trains that run on parallel lines
One on the ground, and one that's in my mind

Mid-life Crisis

I know that I should be a happy man
My health is good, I get three meals a day
I watch the news, but that's all far away
We're living in a green and pleasant land

I have a decent flat, a lovely wife
A son who, most folks say, looks just like me
And so, I can't explain why it should be
I feel there's something missing in my life

Could it be down a path I didn't take
Or something that's behind some secret door
Something different or just something more?
It's just a nagging feeling I can't shake

Living well, of course, is well and good
But in the end, what is it all about
I'm not a true believer, I have doubts
Am I doing everything I should?

As life goes on, and time is slipping by
I do the things I do, but don't know why

Points on a Line

When I was young, I couldn't quite conceive
Of being quite as old as I am now
Actually, it's still hard to believe
Aging really shouldn't be allowed

I looked at those much bigger than me then
As creatures from another universe
I really didn't want to be like them
Slow and grumpy, that would be the worst

Life is a parade in time and space
And no one gets to pass the same point twice
Proceeding at a slow and steady pace
Sometimes it's hard, but usually it's nice

We stand at different points along the line
From where I'm standing now, it looks just fine

The Interface Between Nature and Man

Unhurriedly, the shallow river flows
In its own time, across the old stone weir
It's muddy at the top, but down below
The water is miraculously clear

The campground on its bank is filled with cars
Families with their tents and caravans
The borderline is anywhere you are
Between the world of nature and of man

Looking up, upon the towering hill
Sheep are grazing, then there are the woods
The sheep look like they're almost standing still
Change comes slowly, everything is good

The sun goes down, the shallow river flows
The stars come out, and that's the way it goes

Geometry

In winter, when the trees are shorn and bare
And all the leaves have fallen to the floor
We see what's there behind what isn't there
It was, but now it isn't any more

The skeletons of trees now stand exposed
The patterns of their branches are revealed
Against the heartless sky is juxtaposed
Their naked beauty and their stark appeal

Their structure, from the branches to the twigs
A monument to fractal symmetry
The smaller forms that duplicate the big
The way things are, the way they'll always be

The view is clear, the air is cold and fresh
Winter shows us nature in the flesh

Soliloquy

The very blankness of the empty page
Is begging for some words to fill it up
As the water's destined for the cup
And so I sit and type some words of rage

Bitter words, of anger unexpressed
Words of pain, and sorrow for the dead
We sit and write our hollow words instead
Of doing what we know would bring us rest

The answer to the question Hamlet posed
To be, or not to be, is clear enough
Even when things get a little rough
I'd never want to bring it to a close

Though life is sometimes hard, it's understood
Compared to the alternative, it's good

Reciprocation

Sometimes it seems a parent's job is one
Of stopping kids from having too much fun
We will not let them climb up on the shelves
Perhaps because we can't do that ourselves

We will not let them touch a lot of stuff
It makes a child's life extremely rough
No knives, no scissors, none of life's great joys
We try to make them play with boring toys

But, sometimes it also works the other way
There are things that we can't do or say
Children copy everything they see
And that is not how we want them to be

So, everything is working out just fine
Because the children keep adults in line

Rules of a Sonnet

A cherry pie is more than just some food
That, by happenstance, has cherries on it
So, when poets ply their poetude
Not every piece they pen is called a sonnet

Of syllables there must be 10 per line
Perhaps eleven if one of them is weak
You might get away with only nine
But ten's the magic number you should seek

Just 14 lines, or 18 is O.K.
And it must rhyme, like this: aabb
abab or else abba
You've got choices, any of those three

Iambic meter is the hardest part
But necessary to this form of art

Rinat's Poem

The moon above is hard and bitter cold
Its shining face is just reflected light
But there it is, a beacon in the night
Dispelling deepest dark with brilliant gold

A plant can be a flower or a weed
A sign of our affection, or a waste
But which is which depends upon our taste
Their meaning is according to our need

The heart is just a bloody pump, it's clear
The seat of our emotions is the mind
The poets lie, but still, somehow, I find
My heart beats faster every time you're near

Science can explain a lot of stuff
Artificial hearts can beat as well
And chemicals replace the flowers smell
But explanations somehow aren't enough

When we want to write a poem of love
It's hearts and flowers, and the moon above

Dandelions

When dandelions bloom throughout the land
Like golden jewels scattered on the lawn
We know that summer days are close at hand
Spring is here, and winter is long gone

But as I wander down these city streets
Concrete canyons flanked by walls of gray
There is no soft, green grass beneath my feet
The day looks much like any other day

But even though we've blanketed the earth
With concrete, plastic, glass and all the rest
Spring is joy, and light, and love, and birth
Spring springs back, spring cannot be suppressed

The tables that pour out of the café's
And sprout like flowers on each city street
To take advantage of the sunny days
Are omens no less certain, nor less sweet

Where dandelions are a rarer thing
There are other, urban signs of spring

The Cynic

One morning, barely half awake, I heard
The sound of music, coming from the trees
Gently borne upon the summer breeze
But all that I could think was "stupid birds"

That evening I was walking through the park
And saw the sunset, brilliant, in the west
Its work was done, and it deserved the rest
But all that came to mind was "now it's dark"

So young and beautiful, well-dressed and rich
My fleeting glance turned to a longing gaze
I tried to think of proper words of praise
But the rhyme that came to mind was "fucking bitch"

I try to write with dignity and class
To clearly use the words as they were meant
At least, without satirical intent
But then a rhyme just bites me in the ass

It's not the story that I meant to tell
But cynicism rhymes so very well

Sam at Five Months

Our son just turned five months the other day
He isn't quite so helpless as before
And he can scoot real well across the floor
As long as there is nothing in his way

He struggles, and he turns from side to side
He gets off balance, or gets turned around
He bumps his little head upon the ground
He hasn't learned to take things in his stride

He doesn't have a stride to take things in
And so he cries, frustrated with the chore
But tries again, and does a little more
And soon, at least at this, I'm sure he'll win

What kind of man he'll be, we still can't tell
But for now, he's doing pretty well

Alienation

I see the other people in the street
Each has an agenda of their own
Each controls the space above their feet
But, ultimately, each is all alone

I look up at the sky that's filled with stars
Each one a quite distinctive point of light
Like fireflies imprisoned in a jar
Like beacon fires shining through the night

Like tiny pebbles on an endless beach
Like a leaf, when millions of them fall
Like drops of water in the sparkling sea
Like the many bricks that make a wall

Sometimes I feel so very, very small
I feel like I'm not even here at all

A Place Beside a Stream

You don't need much; a place beside a stream
The water will accompany your dreams
A rock, out in the desert, far from town
From which to watch the evening sun go down

An isolated beach where no one goes
Where you can let the ocean touch your toes
A place that's far away from city lights
From which to watch the stars come out at night

Just as they have each night since time began
Long before the troubled time of man
'Cause every day we're hearing more and more
Of politics and violence and war

It's good to get away from all the din
And see the world the way it's always been

Fractals of the Human Race

We go, we shop, we choose, perhaps we vote
Everything we do defines the day
And future generations will take note
Of what we did, and what we didn't say

And everything we do or do not do
Are things which lead, in turn, to other things
And every moment we begin anew
After butterflies have flapped their wings

It seems, sometimes, that things are on a course
That can't be changed, no matter how we act
But each of us exerts a certain force
Everybody matters, it's a fact

Each of our six billion separate souls
Is a fractal of the human whole

I Cannot Stand the Ticking of the Clock

I cannot stand the ticking of the clock
That horrid sound that will not go away
Dividing every minute of each day
Into 60, tiny, little blocks

We try to drown it out with other sounds
Conversation, music, nothing works
Patiently it bides its time, it lurks
When other noises fade, it's still around

Time! The measure of eternity
With which we calculate our time on earth
It's ticking from the moment of our birth
And never, for a moment, are we free

With each tick, each heartbeat, and each breath
We are a second closer to our death

Snow in the Streetlight

It falls, like slow confetti, in the night
Passing through the streetlight's steady glow
For a moment, in their falling flight
There is a sparkle to each flake of snow

Along the row of pillars made of light
The scene's the same, a still and silent show
A beautiful tableau in gold and white
Soft and soothing, sweet, serene, and slow

In the darkness, there is something bright
A shifting scene of particles that flow
One of nature's most amazing sights
Enhanced a bit, but that's the way it goes

The darkness is a background for the light
In the winter, in the city, in the night

The Purposes of Poetry

Some say that poetry should be a spark
A flash of brilliance that ignites a fire
Or a light, to fight against the dark
To clarify, enlighten or inspire

Some say a poem is meant to entertain
Some clever words that make the reader smile
Or maybe cry, for in a world of pain
The flow of tears is also worth our while

Some say a poem is simply to express
All the emotions that the writer feels
The angst, the rage, the sorrow and, I guess
To kindred spirits, that may well appeal

I'm not real sure what poetry is for
For what it's worth, I'll write a couple more

Appreciation

This world we're living on is pretty nice
The land is thick with flowers, grass, and trees
And if you want variety, for spice
There is another world beneath the seas

The mountains are so high, the deserts vast
The meadows are so pleasant and so pretty
A system that, it seems, was meant to last
But everywhere you look, we've built a city

Through the years we've pissed in all the rivers
And through the years we've shat on all the banks
If this great gift was given by a giver
We have a funny way of saying thanks

This world on which we live is pretty great
It would be nice if we'd appreciate it

The Choice

When Dickens wrote "It was the best of times",
He wrote "It was the worst of times" as well
And there's eternal truth within those lines
Life is heaven, but we make it hell

Things are getting better every day
Technology's advancing at a pace
That, in the game of life that we all play
the rules are changing for the human race

Things are getting better, but the curse
That's been with us since history began
Is that they're simultaneously worse
And that's the part that I don't understand

If we all want the future to be good
And smarten up a bit, I think it could

Abundance

The flowers that were painted by Van Gogh
As flowers had one season in the sun
Today, we see them everywhere we go
A million copies of each single one

A captured moment in a summer breeze
Is like the offspring of the Octopi;
A densely populated hive of bees
For each that lives, a thousand more will die

The sights and sounds that hover in the air
A painter's vision early in the morning
Is now immortalized, forever there
As on the canvas, beauty is reborn

Of which, once golden petals were the root
But most attempts do not bear any fruit

The Great Divide

The river winds along the valley floor
It seeks the lowest level it can find
It flows as slow as syrup tends to pour
And everybody goes there to unwind

Canoes attempt to ride the center line
A pair of scissors cutting on the fold
The day is bright, the view is mighty fine
The sun is hot, the water's icy cold

Along the banks the trees are thick and green
Bushes, flowers, cottages and farms
All form a very pleasant summer scene
Where city folk enjoy the rustic charms

Of course the cottage dwellers all have cars
And roads connect to roads connect to roads
There is no upper limit to how far
On either side, the web of things can go

The river marks a line, a great divide
We see infinity on either side

Infinity

We look up at night and see the stars
Tiny dots...the ceiling of the sky
Our predecessors didn't know how far
Away they were, or what, or how, or why?

But now we know that there are other suns
As big and brightly shining as our own
With several planets orbiting each one
Billions of them...we are not alone

And that's just in the galaxy we see
Worlds as endless as the night above
There are billions of other galaxies
And lots of stuff that we know nothing of

Boggling the mind, but what is worse is
There are probably more universes

Earworm

The echo of a song that I once heard
Is bouncing back and forth inside my head
I don't exactly recollect the words
I am not sure exactly what they said

Perhaps it doesn't matter much at all
The buzz of a mosquito in the tent
The moment that I suddenly recall
It bums me out, how little it all meant

If only there were some way we could know
Which things are relevant, and which are not
So we could just forget it, let it go
And get beyond that sticky, clinging spot

It's like a piece of bacon in your teeth
Until it's gone, you won't get any peace

The Road and the Journey

They went out hunting and, at night, came back
The naked apes, across the plains they strode
The steps they took became the beaten track
And those were the precursors of our roads

And then there came the horses, and the carts
Transporting goods and people, place to place
Civilization grew in many parts
And slowly spread across the planet's face

Water couldn't stop the surging host
They built great ships to sail across the seas
And railroads linked things up from coast
And traveling was suddenly a breeze

And then the plodding apes learned how to fly
To explore the air so free and clear
The aeroplanes sailed up into the sky
And rocketships escaped the atmosphere

We've come so far, but we are far from done
The human journey's only just begun

A Summer Day in the Park

The ladies lying on the sun-bathed lawn
Their skin, just like the leaves, absorbs the rays
Butterflies fly by and then they're gone
In the playground, little children play

A wino is passed out from too much wine
Two dogs run back and forth, their favorite game
Among the willow, chestnut, oak and pine
And lots of trees that I don't know their name

People sit on benches there and read
One man hard at work, he cuts the grass
To keep it neat and trim and free of weeds
On the street, trams rumble as they pass

The frivolous, the tragic, the divine
There is life in each and every line

Kaleidoscope

Kaleidoscopes are quite amazing toys
So many different possibilities
Their endless forms of beauty bring us joy
And we're amazed by their complexity

The world is like a big kaleidoscope
The weather changes every single day
Deserts, seas, and pleasant, grassy slopes
And all the different animals at play

There are seasons, there is day and night
There are mountains high and rivers long
Green trees, blues skies, red roses, and snow white
And the wind, that sings a constant song

The earth is an amazing little ball
Each poem is just a fractal of it all

Experience

We work, we play, we eat, we sleep, we dance
We talk, we sing, we read, perhaps we write
We love and we experience romance
We have some laughs but there are times we fight

Our time is filled with lots of different stuff
From when we're born, until the day we die
Of some of it we never get enough
But still, we sometimes stop and wonder...why?

We live our lives to our alloted span
Eighty, maybe ninety years or so
Although we do the very best we can
It's possible that we will never know

No matter how courageously we strive
Exactly what it means to be alive

Light and Dark

The streetlight shining on the placid lake
The water dancing in its steady lights
The streetlight is a camera which takes
A photographic negative of night

The cars continue driving in the dark
Their headlights bore two holes in the unknown
Slicing out a segment, clear and stark
To mark the path by which they need to go

The sunlight shining through the big glass door
To signal the beginning of the day
Casts a golden shadow on the floor
And anything that's sitting in the way

The light of day, so beautiful and fair
Is greater still at times when it is rare

Rivers, Trains, and People

You cannot step into the river twice
It changes from one moment to the next
The old folks claim the past was paradise
But it's as obsolete as ancient text

The idols of our youth grow old and die
The actors and musicians we all know
And we all heave a sweet, nostalgic sigh
But younger ones replaced them long ago

At every step the ritual's observed
Of people getting off and on the train
Their faces change, the balance is preserved
The doors slide shut, the train moves off again

Old folks, young folks, babies, husbands and wives
We are at different stages in our lives

Shakespeare's Sonnet #3, Updated

Shakespeare wrote, in Sonnet #3
And there was wit and wisdom in his rhyme
"Die childless and thy image dies with thee"
And that was fitting to his place and time

The world today's oppressed beneath the weight
Of more than 7 billion pairs of feet
And if those 7 billion replicate
All we'll have is Soylent Green to eat

Write a book if you would make your mark
Paint a painting, make a film or plant a tree
Or dedicate a bench inside a park
With your name upon it for eternity

Live a life of elegance and style
Not everybody needs to have a child

In Vino Veritas

The vinyard lies inside a lake of light
The light is then transformed into the shape
Of perfect little green and purple grapes
So spherical and plump, so firm and tight

The universe is beautiful and good
The grapes are plucked and their life's blood is poured
Into the new containers where it's stored
Venerable casks of ancient wood

From there to glass, the journey's almost done
We lift our glasses, then we have a drink
And that affects the kind of thoughts we think
As we consume the power of the sun

It's more than metaphor to say the wine
May be the means to access the divine

The Ride

Lie on your back on a grassy hillside
Stare straight up into the evening sky
It's the solar system's greatest thrill ride
Seriously, you should give it a try

You should be far away from any city
Far, far away from any city lights
The stars above are really very pretty
But they are best observed in bleakest night

You'll have to stay there for a couple hours
To see that things aren't staying in one place
Embrace the void, and you will feel the power
The vast and awesome emptiness of space

You'll feel the earth as it is spinning round
Alone, in empty space, without a sound

The Origin of Painting

The hungry tribe was huddled in the cave
Sheltered from the weather and the lions
They were timid more than they were brave
They had to be, to live in those environs

When someone got some gunk upon their hand
A bit of ochrous clay, and slightly damp
They rubbed it off against the nearest wall
And noticed that it left a ragged stamp

Then, in the light of fire dimmed by smoke
They altered it with fingers and with sticks
Perhaps, at first, they thought it quite a joke
A game, perhaps, a sort of magic trick

But once you've killed the bison in your brain
Then you can kill the bison on the plain

Legacy

This is meant for future generations
It is to them this humble book belongs
The past is gone, despite our lamentations
And the present isn't going to last for long

When I was young, I thought the world would change
I felt our true potential was untapped
The future could be perfectly arranged
And all good hippie children would adapt

And so it changed, but not as I'd foreseen
History's a complex situation
We didn't do so well, is what I mean
So this is meant for future generations

My kids, my kids' kids, and my kids' kids' kids
I hope that you do better than we did

The Greatness of the Common Man

As individuals, we're not that great
Most people never play the starring role
A beauty queen, a major head of state
Or thrill the masses with the winning goal

And yet, the people who make up the crowd
The ones for whom the players play the game
They raise their voice as one, and it is loud
They are the source of that one athlete's fame

In Greece, they make a special sort of wine
From what is at the bottom of the kegs
Inelegant, for sure, but still divine
There is a lot of flavor in the dregs

There are times when we can all be proud
Just to be a person in the crowd

I wonder

I wonder what is going through their minds
These people who I see upon the train
What hopes, what dreams, what plans, what grand
designs
What joys, what fears, what pleasures and what pains

Are their thoughts formed in pictures or in sounds
Could there be some who do not dream at all
But concentrate on what is right around
And focus on not bumping into walls?

Statistically, I guess, it must be so
But at the Bell Curve's positive extreme
Some must have mental images that glow
With vivid fantasies and golden dreams

I wonder what is going through their minds
And wonder if they wonder what's in mine

Let There Be Light...

God said "Let there be light" and there was light
It's written in the book of Genesis
And lo, the Universe came to exist
And daytime was divided from the night

Science has a slightly different angle
A mass of matter, gathered in one spot
Everything that is, and that's a lot
Exploded in a massive bloody bang

The universe exists, so we are blessed
And when all our senses are in play
We know the world in more than just one way
And truth is truth, however it's expressed

I'm convinced the Bible's only fiction
But, in fact, there is no contradiction

Collective Consciousness

We are 6 billion people, more or less
And see things through 6 billion sets of eyes
So, it should really come as no surprise
Our politics is such a fucking mess

We have different values, different goals
Different tastes and different points of view
Though each one thinks the things he thinks are true
Each one is only playing out one role

Some are beautiful and telegenic
Though some may go against the given grain
Most of us, alone, are fairly sane
Collectively, we are a schizophrenic

If we work together we can be great
If we do not, we'll have a lesser fate

Fog

One day while I was walking in the fog
So thick that I was very nearly blind
I heard a bark, but it was just a dog
And not the werewolf that was in my mind

I heard the hum of tires coming near
And saw two orbs of yellow on the gray
Though not the giant juggernaut I feared
Nonetheless, I stepped out of the way

A square of light that hovered in the air
Was probably a cottage on a hill
It also could have been a castle there
In the fog there was no way to tell

It's when our vision is a bit impaired
We see the things that aren't really there

Sonnet from 30,000 Feet

At 30,000 feet above the ground
Encased within a hollow tube of steel
They sit, and read, and chat, and have their meal
And seldom even bother looking down

There's something here unnatural, unreal
Separated from all earthly things
Suspended here on artificial wings
Feet touch no ground, no road's beneath the wheels

Mankind, who was by nature born to walk
(But, nature being not enough for man)
Soars higher than the eagle, than the hawk
And doesn't even wonder that he can

At 30,000 feet up in the sky
Behold! The mite of man who's learned to fly

Elegy for my Father

My father's dead, I got the news today
He was fit for a man of seventy nine
And we all thought that he was doing fine
A sudden stroke just took his life away

Nine grandkids, seven kids, a loving wife
The buildings that he built, the war he won
One has to say, when all is said and done
He led a fruitful and rewarding life

I went walking through the Old Town Square
Here in this ancient, European town
And saw the tourists looking all around
At all the tourist trinkets that are there

I saw boys dressed up like girls and girls like clowns
Ringing bells and asking me for change
Laughing, and perhaps they found it strange
That I wept as I tossed in a couple crowns

With every step we take, each single breath
It's reaffirmed: Life doesn't stop for death

Perhaps

Perhaps the bird who's singing in the trees
Doesn't see himself as wild and free
But a diligent defender of the nest
Because that is the place he loves the best

Perhaps the reason turtles move so slow
Is that they really have no place to go
Perhaps they're shy, and life inside their shell
Is comfortable, and suits them very well

Perhaps the fish that's swimming in the sea
Knows nothing of what was, or what will be
A limited existence, we might say
But for the little fish, perhaps, O.K.

Perhaps there is a reason things are so
I say perhaps, of course, 'cause I don't know

Dangerous Elements

The amber fields of gently waving grain
Vast, majestic, beautiful and still
Until the wind comes sweeping down the plain
Howling, and with clear intent to kill

The angry sky is storming 'cross the ground
Consuming everything that's in its course
It spins around and faster spins around
Till it becomes a solid wall of force

The forest fires leap from tree to tree
Tectonic plates can split the ground in two
The rolling river rises steadily
It seems that there is little we can do

Earth and water, fire and raging air
These are still things of which we should beware

The Inherent Futility of Poetry

The poet's job is futile, for, at best
Only other poets are impressed
The quest, from the beginning, is absurd
To think we can define the world with words

A stream does not require words to flow
The plants do not require words to grow
The Sun, without our words, would shine as bright
And still be hidden from our eyes at night

And how much less the sentiments we feel
Need our hollow words to make them real
Love and passion, sorrow, fear and rage
Gain nothing from expression on the page

They have been with us from the dawn of time
Though languages have changed, and feeble rhymes
Dissovle into a meaningless refrain
That makes the very effort seem insane

Still, I present to you the world I see
In all its madness and absurdity

Dawn and Dusk

Though different both in meaning and in name
The dawn and dusk look very much the same
An optimistic pink Atlantic hue
Foreshadowing the deep Pacific blue

Think of them as covers to a book
Open it at dawn and take a look
The letters are quite clear and plain to see
Though most of us just scan, and never read

Letters forming words in plants that grow
Expressing in a way they seem to know
The sunlight spells it out so very plain
In phrases which describe the magic chain

A consciousness is flowing in the streams
There, for us to see, in golden beams

Earthly Powers

We have within our hearts both love and hate
The power to destroy or to create
Destruction is the easier of the two
And seems to be what we prefer to do

We have a thumb so we can grasp and clutch
Manipulate and change the things we touch
The touch of man is felt across the land
As greedy eyes are fed by willing hands

We have within our minds the power to plan
Just what will be the future state of man
Homelessness and famine, war and woe
There is no law that says it must be so

The world could be a better kind of place
If we but willed that that should be the case

Sonnet on Buckminster Fuller's Definition of Fire

The leaves absorb their living from the sun
A process that is hard to comprehend
Of energy to matter, but the end
Results a standing forest when they're done

A forest filled with trees that grow and die
And leave their scattered trunks upon the ground
Abandoned treasure, waiting to be found
We gather logs to put them on the fire

Fire flies, it's such a pretty sight
From logs and twigs and other burning things
As curved and graceful as a Phoenix' wings
The flames are flying up into the night

Each curving wingtip shoots a spray of sparks
Like champagne bubbles rising in a glass
Their brief illumination soon will pass
Their heat disperses in the cold and dark

The sun, which was wrapped up inside a tree
Unwraps itself, and once again is free

In Photographs

In photographs we keep upon the shelves
In heroes we portray in films and books
In each reflective surface that we look
We seek a sharper image of ourselves

But should we wish for more than just a glance
And dare to leave the valley of the blind
We must accept the image that we find
We have to be prepared to take a chance

Reality itself is not so bad
Our imperfections only give us some
Things for us to try and overcome
There is no point at all in getting mad

When imperfections fail to disappear
We can't, in fairness, blame it on the mirror

Restraint

How often have we slowly walked away
Pondering the thing we meant to say
And looking back with retroactive dread
Upon the thing we actually said?

Things are different now in cyberspace
Because we are not meeting face to face
We can think a bit before we write
We mostly don't but, nonetheless, we might

While scrolling through the comments on the screen
So many are so ignorant and mean
False assumptions, hate and blatant lies
The trick is to compose a good reply

"Fuck you, retard!" Sounds O.K. at first
But out of all our choices, it's the worst

Smoothed Glass

A broken bottle left upon the beach
Small and jagged pieces scattered 'round
Lying with the pebbles on the ground
Left carelessly within Poseidon's reach

Garbage left at Paradise's door
Granted time and tide and left alone
The waves will turn the glass to polished stone
Green as jade and glistening on the shore

The mother's touch is there in every breeze
As paper turns to pulp in pelting rain
And grass breaks through the sidewalk once again
The wind will brush the soot from off the trees

The magpie and the beetle and the ant
Will do their part, not knowing what they do
To clear the old, and make way for the new
And fire and flood will finish what they can't

Though scars run deep and wounds are very real
Earth will survive us and, in time, will heal

In Memoriam

We saw the flames, the smoke and the debris
But did not feel the sidewalk as it shook
We only had the pictures that they took
As filtered through the screen of our TV

We didn't breathe the clouds of rolling dust
We didn't feel the panic in the air
We do not bear the burden of despair
That all the victim's families now must

We sat, transfixed, and listened to the news
The newsmen soon ran out of things to say
We called our friends to see they were O.K.
There wasn't that much else that we could do

Words of sorrow never will erase
The horror and the grief, perhaps instead
We should dedicate our living to the dead
And try to make the world a better place

Today, the unbelievable is true
But life goes on, 'cause what else can it do?

That Bloody Flag

I'm American, and I am ashamed
When I hear the stupid things that people say
A couple thousand dead'll be O.K.
You seem to think that it's some kind of game

Those are real people that you plan to kill
Real bodies will be lying in the street
Real burns upon real skin won't look so neat
As the CNN half hour version will

You wave your flags and talk a lot of crap
About our great, heroic, fighting boys
Playing with their billion dollar toys
As you move your pins around a paper map

I see a wave of flags across the sky
And know that children are about to die

Plato's Cave Revisited

How fortunate our history begins
Upon a world which, neat as clockwork, spins
We see our world, as lighted by the sun
The fine detail with which the work was done

And then, at night, the blinding light goes out
And certainty gives way to dark and doubt
But yet, though all the world may be concealed
It's then that vast eternity's revealed

We get a new perspective of our place
By looking on the sea of time and space:
The Yin and Yang, the in and out, the two
It's fortunate that we have had this view

Our vision is no better than our sight
Obscured by dark, or blinded by the light

Valentine's Day

Upon this very arbitrary day
When every husband has to find a way
To show the flame of love's still burning true
I do not know what I can give to you

I don't have cash to buy a diamond ring
A necklace or some other blingy thing
To show you that you are my special girl
The banks have all the money in the world

Every day, there's so much that you give
Without you, I don't know how I would live
And yet, this little poem will have to do
To let you know how much I treasure you

Upon this day I pledge to you, my wife
My heart is yours, and will be all my life

Hollywood and Mulholland Drive

The candles give the meaning to the cake
The pine trees are reflected in the lake
Each generation resurrects the last
The future is a mirror of the past

A classic work performed upon the stage
Reflects what is reflected on the page
Words so poignant, music so sublime
Are not decreased with distance or with time

The image of the whole that meets the eye
As chaos yields to order by-and-by
When looking at the city from a height
The clutter of the day erased by night

A bright reflection of the cosmic plan
A sky of stars spread out across the land

A Single Grain of Sand

A single grain of sand has little weight
The most that it can do is irritate
Somewhere inside your shorts that's hard to reach
But lots of them make up a lovely beach

Snow requires more than just one flake
A single word does not a novel make
A single thread does not create a net
A solitary voice a choir, but yet

The quality of each and every one
Affects the whole, when all is said and done
A single rotten plank can ruin a boat
And make it quite impossible to float

You cannot have a money making store
Whose shelves are stocked with useless rubbish, or
A healthy forest made of sickly trees
People are a lot like that, if we

Were all just slightly better than we are
The world would be a better place by far

To a Newborn

I don't recall at all when I was born
My first impressions of this crazy world
What sights before my virgin eyes unfurled
I don't recall a single thing before

I was four, or maybe even five
I don't remember learning how to walk
I don't remember learning how to talk
Or the moment I first knew I was alive

And now we see you at that early stage
You look at us and don't know who we are
In fact, you don't know anything so far
Your mind an as yet unimprinted page

The slate is blank; the screen is free and clear
But, 1st impressions mean a lot, we know
And we trust you'll understand them as you grow
You'll see it in our faces, and you'll hear

It in our voices, feel it in our touch
Your parents love you very, very much

Sudoku

Sudoko puzzles are a lot of fun
987654321
The symmetrical arrangement of the squares
Every number fits in there somewhere

Some people (I confess I am not one)
Arrange their lives like that, and get things done
A place for everything within their space
And all those things fit neatly into place

It takes all kinds to make a world, Lord knows
And it's a better method, I suppose
But things arranged in lines are rather tame
And leave us yearning for the burning flame

The howling of the wind, the crashing waves
These are the things the human spirit craves

If There's a God

If there's a God, then how can we explain
This world of evil, suffering and pain
Fear and famine, hate, disease and war?
Why are some folks rich, and others poor?

It isn't quite convincing just to say
The big guy works in strange and secret ways
If this is what he does with total power
It's safe to say his motives aren't ours

But still, we have the forests and the streams
And the better world we're building in our dreams
Could be that he exists and doesn't care
Or it could be he really isn't there

In this, as in a random universe
Things could be better, or they could be worse

Dear CNN

You didn't want the pictures to be seen
Of mangled bodies lying in the sand
It wasn't suited to the family screen
In living rooms across our Christian land

Interviews with soldiers were O.K.
Images to fill our souls with pride
Those friendly faces from the U.S.A.
Who could deny that God was on our side?

And now they say it's over and we won
We should be proud, we should be standing tall
It's time for celebration and for fun
'Cause it was fairly easy, after all

Without the pictures, fresh, inside our heads
How quickly we forget about the dead

Centigrade

At two degrees, the rain comes pelting down
The leaves are gone; the trees are stark and bare
That, months ago, were full and green and fair
The sky is gray, the earth a muddy brown

The people run for shelter from the rain
And cringe to feel its cold and clammy touch
Slightly warmer wouldn't matter much
But slightly colder, then you see a change

The chilling drops turn into crystal flakes
Pretty, soft and gentle, almost dry
That fall like slow confetti from the sky
Amazing, what a difference it makes

At zero, nature goes into reverse
And things get better, once they've gotten worse

January

I feel a cold wind blowing from the west
Whose bitter breath will turn the world to stone
The kind of cold that chills you to the bone
If you're outside, no matter how you're dressed

The bright and hopeful summer faded fast
A time of laughter and a time of fun
A time of hope, when things were getting done
We should have known it was too good to last

The rings of power all have been secured
The emperor, his congress and his court
Now rule, without dissent, and will resort
To any means, so power is assured

The wind is blowing, it's dark and scary
Hell will freeze over, this January

Mandela

We had the first snow of the year today
Appropriate, it marked the moment when
A legendary leader passed away
The world will never be the same again

Born into a hot and troubled land
He studied hard and always did his best
To get along in life and understand
Became a lawyer, helping the oppressed

For 27 years he was in jail
But through it all stayed faithful to his cause
They limited his visits and his mail
But in the end he won and changed the laws

He left hope that we can live together
In all lands and in all kinds of weather

Family of Man

Scientists have recently revealed
A bit of human geneaology
From way, way back in our prehistory
Which prior to this point had been concealed

From tracing back our DNA they know
One man was the granddaddy of us all
In Africa, a long, long time ago
Back when the human gene pool was still small

There were other lines he interbred with
Some, perhaps, are with us to this day
But everybody who you go to bed with
Is related to you in some way

From this, the thing we need to understand
Is that we are a family of man

Enter the Garbagemen

The garbagemen are up before the dawn
We hear the clashing gears and then the whine
The clash of gears again, and then they're gone
Then we go back to bed and all is fine

In the country it's the cock who crows
At first perception of the coming dawn
Some people rise, but they're still moving slow
And there are beads of dew upon the lawn

These scenes, repeating, constant as a GIF
The line of light moves forward zone by zone
So steadily it almost seems as if
It's the lighting of the stage that sets the tone

The sky is changing color as we spin
And this is how another day begins

Waking Up Slow

I take my time re-entering real time
If you wake up and jump right out of bed
You shatter what was tranquil and sublime
The memory of the dream falls from your head

We close our weary eyes at night to sleep
Our image of the world is redefined
The outside world does not go down that deep
What we can see is all inside our mind

Sometimes we see, again, our childhood face
We may have conversations with the dead
Our actions aren't proscribed by time and space
Sometimes we are someone else instead

It's wonderful, I'd rather not let go
And that is why I'd rather wake up slow

The Worst Thing about Littering

People should be somewhat more ashamed
At all the garbage lying on the ground
There's none but human beings can be blamed
For all the crap that's scattered all around

Apple cores and stuff will blend right in
Feed the insects, all part of the chain
Scraps of paper that never reach the bin
Eventually are broken down by rain

Plastic bottles, butts of cigarettes
Look like they're a scalp disease of grass
We find the sight a bit disturbing, yet
Eventually, the groundskeeper will pass

BUT, a plastic bag caught up in a tree
Can stay up there for all eternity

Inevitability

Moving, moving everywhere we go
A conga line of farting, metal beasts
Sometimes stopped, and sometimes moving slow
Two lanes, from North to South, from West to East

They never stop; they roll by night and day
And have been ever since, at least, my birth
Obliviously smiling on their way
While sucking up the juices of the Earth

Which scientists have told us, there's no doubt
Every minute, every single mile
We're closer to the oil running out
And they've been saying this for quite a while

When we run out of oil, by and by
Everybody's going to act surprised

Mustek

Trudging through the corridor at Mustek
The daily hordes of people bravely march
Hurriedly, and you can hear their shoes peck
Peck, peck, peck they echo around the arch

Some of them are ambling, most just gotta
Get to work, a meeting, or a class
It's an everyday spartakiada
The individuals make up the mass

Like the power of a raging river
Like a current surging through a wire
Alone, we don't have that much to deliver
All together, we're as fierce as fire

This people power is quite exciting
On the other hand, a little frightening

CWTC7

Admittedly, I'm not an engineer
An architect or anything like that
But, nonetheless, to me it seems quite clear
Upright columns don't get squashed down flat

They fall down to the left or to the right
They are not pancakes, that's a lot of crap
They don't get zapped and vanish from our sight
There had to have been something made them snap

Building 7 was not so far away
And not built quite the same as 1 and 2
But just the same, upon that fateful day
Fell straight down (as buildings seldom do)

Two planes could not have made 3 buildings fall
That just does not make any sense at all

In the Land of Metaphors

A seed can be a metaphor for birth
The night can be a metaphor for death
A word can be worth more than what it's worth
The wind can be a metaphor for breath

Or for change, as it sweeps across the land
The birds that surf its wave are metaphors
They stretch their wings out to their fullest span
We watch them and our own self-image soars

The path starts in this world in which we're caught
It is laid out like stones across a stream
The other side is in the world of thought
We do our best to navigate the dream

We draw the map, so that we can explore
We jump from metaphor to metaphor

The Leering Poet

There is a world contained inside each mind
Not bound by laws of physicality
Unique and individually designed
Different versions of reality

But as we live and breathe in time and space
We're always seeking hoping that we'll find
A magic portal or an interface
Enlightenment, so we will be less blind

The words we speak, or put upon the page
Are a door between these worlds, a link
They are a point, a step, a crucial stage
In making real the thoughts we merely think

The leering poet's standing by the gate
Hey! Come on, people. Let's communicate.

Dreamers and Poets

You're late to class, and you're not wearing pants
The monster chases you right off a cliff
You meet a kangaroo who wants to dance
The scene plays out inside your minds as if

Things could turn into other things at will
Suddenly a flower becomes a fire
A flaming surge of passion, it's a thrill
And a beacon of your true desire

Everything we see inside our mind
Behind our eyes, when they are closed at night
Represents the things we're trying to fight
On our endless journey into the night

Juggling symbols, metaphors, and memes
It seems we all are poets, in our dreams

Respect

Most modern poets have disdain for rhyme
And some treat meter with contempt as well
They seem to think tradition is a crime
But here I am, and they can go to hell

You take away these things, and all you've got
Is someone talking, just a bunch of words
They say that it's a poem, but it's not
More than random phrases we all have heard

The things that people say when people meet
Some rambling sentences where they digress
The things that people shout across the street
Can that be poetry? O.K., I guess

Call it what you like, then, I'm not fighting
But what do you call what I am writing?

Viral Smiles

To smile, or not to smile, you have a choice
Of course, a bit depends upon your mood
But in your choice of mood you have a voice
And that depends upon your attitude

It may seem hypocritical, a bit
To smile when your mood is dark and gray
And everything you had has turned to shit
But it will help to get you through the day

And like the maple seed upon the breeze
Like Nutella on a piece of bread
A smile is just as pleasant as you please
Both easily and very swiftly spread

Just flex a couple muscles in your face
And you can make the world a better place

New World

The thoughts that are contained inside my head
Do not have color, texture, scent, or weight
Or anything that's physical, instead
They exist within a different state

That which we think of as imaginary
Fantastic, metaphorical, sublime
Is becoming real, its presence carries
Into physical space, and current time

Our fingers hit the keyboard and they send
Our minds constructions out into the air
A thin, but never ending thread that tends
To form a link with other threads out there

These interlinking threads soon form a net
And that's about as real as real can get

Sweet Spot

Some people spend a lot of time in cars
Some the great outdoors, exotic places
Some inhabit dark and smoky bars
But millions spend their days in office spaces

Clean, so very clean, so stark, so bright
A total contrast to most people's flats
The pictures on the walls lined up just right
No piles of dirty clothes, no shedding cat

The girls in cubicles, all in a line
The cute receptionist, who smiles so sweet
Their typing fingers, manicured so fine
Oh, what I'd give, to be in their spread sheets

Intended for the art of making money
Nonetheless, most offices ooze honey

The Pace of Progress

Every day, at quite a frightful pace
Scientists find new planets out in space
Another thing they're finding frequently
Is different forms of life beneath the sea

Artificial eyes to help the blind
Computers that are merging with the mind
New paradigms are coming into play
Almost each and every single day

3-D printers and elevated trains
Above the fields of amber, waving grain
Each new thing that we find fits into place
The scope increases, and so does the pace

When we reach information overload
Will civilization flower, or explode?

Ballet Lessons

I drop my daughter off at ballet class
And then I have about an hour to wait
To master the sweet art of how to pass
This surplus patch of time would be real great

My kindle has some books I haven't read
But machines don't like me very much, you know
It's always then the batteries go dead
Coincidence? Somehow, I don't think so

Some can just sit and sit and blankly stare
To me, that is a tragedy, a sin
Life is too short; there is no time to spare
Empty moments beg to be filled in

If I can write a couple decent lines
It won't have been a total waste of time

Breakfast

Two eggs that look like daisies on a plate
Two thick slabs of tender, succulent ham
Two pieces toast, and that works out just great
One to mop up the yolks and one for jam

Some fried potatoes, hot and golden brown
To break the fast, and feed our human greed
Before we struggle with the world around
It's coffee; it's the coffee that we need

Praise the pig as you consume his flesh!
The amber fields of grain that grew the flour!
Praise the eggs, for they are new and fresh!
From all of this, we draw our daily power

To face the day, to deal with what is real
Breakfast is my very favorite meal

The Universe Inside Your Head

I see your face; I look into your eyes
They are the windows of the soul, it's said
No way! No matter how hard I might try
I cannot see the thoughts inside your head

The curtains drawn, there's nothing we can see
Behind the barrier of skin and skull
In that forbidden city, all is free
Non-physical, unbound, dynamic, full

The body's just a vehicle we use
Hands to gesture with, and a mouth to speak
With so much we could say, why do we choose
To keep our words so mild and so meek?

The world in which we live is incomplete
When we speak out, two universes meet

Manifesto

The perfect world we're trying to create
Quite humbly I submit, we should resolve
To, as best we can, approximate
The natural one, on which we all evolved

The water that is flowing in the streams
Should be crystal clear and fit to drink
The golden past inspires our present dreams
And to the golden future is a link

As we grow up we still must feel our roots
Biology cannot be put aside
The herbs, the grains, the vegetables, the fruit
Should grow in great abundance far and wide

The air should not be filled with toxic fumes
We should be able to enjoy the breeze
We can choose a future dark and gloomy
Or we can choose a future filled with trees

To make the future sunny, bright, and breezy
Actually, should be rather easy

The Lure of Femininity

I do not understand why girls like boys
We're dirty, crude, and sometimes not too bright
We're indiscrete; we make a lot of noise
Aggressive, and some even like to fight

But women, oh, a woman's skin is smooth
The merest touch is heavenly delight
Their soft and flowing hair, the way they move
A little to the left and to the right

Boys don't look at paintings on the walls
We piss upon the flowers in the park
Sometimes, we need a respite from it all
A bit of light in all that's mean and dark

Around the world, in every town and city
Boys love girls because they are so pretty

City of Art

Writers walk around its neighborhoods
Photographers take photographs like mad
Some of them, sometimes, create something good
And we can just ignore whatever's bad

There are galleries everywhere you go
And some of them are restaurants and cafés
There are events where living artists show
The work that they are working on that day

The art of architecture's everywhere
Bands make music in the pubs after dark
There are buskers in the city's squares
And the birds are singing sweetly in the park

Here, there is a certain atmosphere
That inspires us to something higher
Especially at night, the light shines clear
On the gold and silver domes and spires

Most cities just exist, but have no heart
Prague, sweet Prague, is a city made of art

Printed in Great Britain
by Amazon.co.uk, Ltd.,
Marston Gate.